I Can Write Poems

Poems

Anita Ganeri

www.raintreepublishers.co.uk
Visit our website to find out more information about Raintree books.

To order:
☎ Phone 0845 6044371
🖹 Fax +44 (0) 1865 312263
🖳 Email myorders@raintreepublishers.co.uk

Customers from outside the UK please telephone +44 1865 312262

Raintree is an imprint of Capstone Global Library Limited, a company incorporated in England and Wales having its registered office at 7 Pilgrim Street, London, EC4V 6LB – Registered company number: 6695582

Edited by Daniel Nunn, Rebecca Rissman, and Sian Smith
Designed by Victoria Allen
Picture research by Elizabeth Alexander
Original illustrations © Capstone Global Library Ltd 2013
Illustrated by Victoria Allen and Darren Lingard
Production by Victoria Fitzgerald
Originated by Capstone Global Library Ltd
Printed and bound in China by Leo Paper Products Ltd

ISBN 978 1 406 23833 4
16 15 14 13 12
10 9 8 7 6 5 4 3 2 1

British Library Cataloguing in Publication Data
Ganeri, Anita, 1961-
  Poems. -- (I can write)
  1. Poetry--Juvenile literature. 2. Poetry--Authorship--Juvenile literature.
  I. Title II. Series
  808.1-dc23

Acknowledgements
We would like to thank the following for permission to reproduce photographs and artworks: Alamy pp.5 (© Geraint Lewis), 6 (© Art Directors & TRIP), 7 (© Jon Arnold Images Ltd), 8 (© Lebrecht Music and Arts Photo Library), 9 (© V&A Images), 26 (© Lebrecht Music and Arts Photo Library); Shutterstock pp.10 (© Rainer Plendl), 12 (© Elena Schweitzer), 12 (© M. Unal Ozmen), 12 (© joingate), 13 (© Allaua), 14 (© Tony Campbell), 15 (© Alexander Ryabintsev), 15 (© Inc), 16 (© Pushkin), 16 (© Cienpies Design), 17 (© Meganom), 17 (© HORUSHKIN), 18 (© Jim Agronick), 19 (© Eric Isselée), 20 (© PILart), 21 (© twentyfourworks), 21 (© antart), 21 (© Skocko), 23 (© Amy Tseng), 24 (© Vasyl Helevachuk), 25 (© Oleksii Sagitov), 27 (© Klara Viskova); Superstock pp.4 (© fStop), 11 (© Fancy Collection).

Every effort has been made to contact copyright holders of material reproduced in this book. Any omissions will be rectified in subsequent printings if notice is given to the publisher.

Disclaimer
All the internet addresses (URLs) given in this book were valid at the time of going to press. However, due to the dynamic nature of the internet, some addresses may have changed, or sites may have changed or ceased to exist since publication. While the author and publisher regret any inconvenience this may cause readers, no responsibility for any such changes can be accepted by either the author or the publisher.

Contents

Some words are shown in bold, **like this**. You can find out what they mean in the glossary on page 30.

What is writing?

You are writing when you put words on paper or a computer screen. Learning to write clearly makes it easier for readers to understand what you mean.

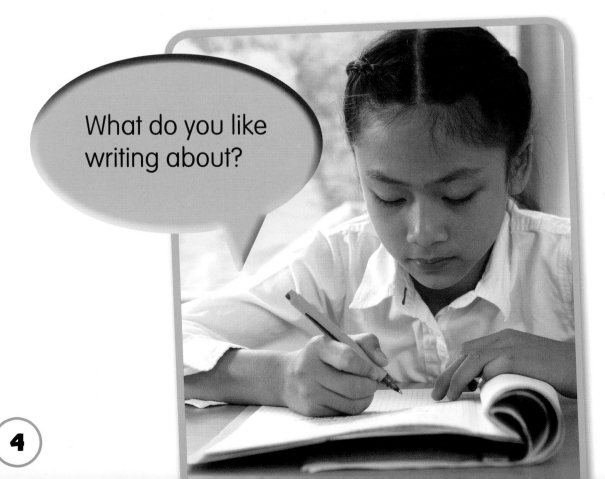

What do you like writing about?

Michael Rosen is a famous poet. A poet writes poems.

There are many different types of writing. This book is about poems. Poems can be **fiction**. This means that they are about made-up things. Some poems can be **non-fiction**. This means that they are about real things.

What are poems?

A poem is a piece of writing that is usually written in **lines**. Several lines make up a **verse**. Poems often **rhyme**. They often use words that show feelings or thoughts.

Writing poems can be fun.

Firework

F orgetting the time
I rush to see
R ockets blasting in the sky
e very one with a Bang
W hen will I remember this time?
o range slashes and pink
r ed and yellow, green and blue
k ee hon and Hollyk were watching too
S ee you next year, good night!

Alexia

These dancers are acting out a poem.

For many years, poems were not written down. People learned them by heart. Then they told or acted the poems out loud. This still happens in some parts of the world.

Different poems

There are lots of different types of poems. There are nursery rhymes, **riddles**, **limericks**, and **haikus**. Which type of poem do you like reading best?

Nursery rhymes are a kind of poem.

JACK·AND·JILL WENT·UP·THE·HILL TO·FETCH·A·PAIL·OF·WATER

Edward Lear was an artist and a poet.

It is best to start off writing the sort of poem that you enjoy reading. If you like limericks, read lots of limericks written by other authors, such as Edward Lear.

Getting ideas

Ideas for poems can come from anywhere! Let your imagination start working or let your feelings tell you what to write. You can also turn memories and dreams into poems.

What are you thinking or feeling?

Jot down any good ideas as soon as you have them.

Keep a notebook and pen with you.
Then you can jot down any ideas that
you have. Scribble down rough notes.
You can write them up properly later on.

Planning a poem

Thinking up a poem can be hard. Here are some tips to help you. Take a word and then note down anything you know or feel about it. This is called **mind mapping**.

This is a mind map for the word 'summer'.

SUMMER

holidays

seaside

feeling happy

ice cream

sunny weather

Another way is to draw a diagram called a spidergram. Write a key word in a circle. Then write lots of connected words or ideas around the outside.

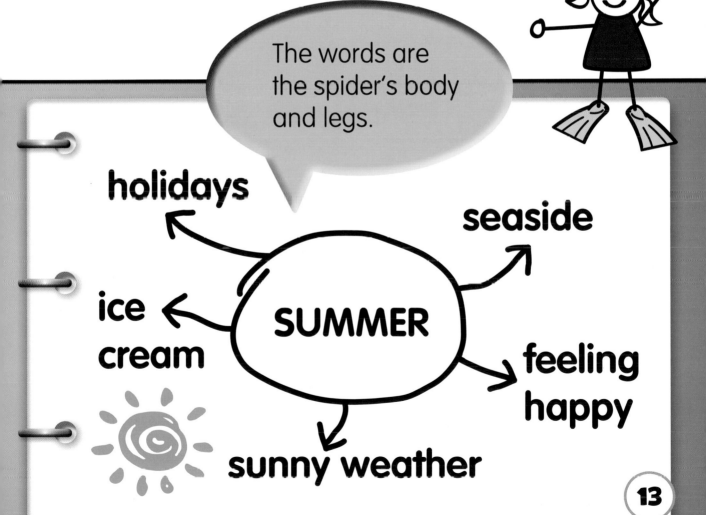

The words are the spider's body and legs.

holidays

seaside

ice cream

SUMMER

feeling happy

sunny weather

Rhyme and rhythm

Many poems **rhyme**. This means that words at the end of **lines** sound the same. Read the poem below. Can you think of a rhyming word, or words, to fill the gap?

My cat

I am black and furry.
I like to sleep all day!
But if I see a dog go by,
I like to run _____.

You could say 'away' or 'and play'.

Many poems have a **beat** or **rhythm**. This makes them sound more like songs when you read them out loud. It also makes the poems easier to read out loud.

Read this poem and clap out the rhythm.

Rain, rain, go away,
Come again another day.

Words and sounds

It is important to think about how words sound when you are writing a poem. The sound can help with the **rhyme** and **rhythm**. Here are some words that sound like their meanings.

Can you think of any more?

fizz

hiss

cheep

whisper

bang

Try using lots of words that start with the same letter. This is called **alliteration** (say 'al-it-er-ay-shun').

You can use alliteration to create interesting sounds in your poem.

The _c_razy _c_reature _c_rawled into the _c_reepy _c_astle.

Acrostic poems

An acrostic is a simple type of poem. You write the letters of a word down the side of the page. Then the first letter of each **line** starts a word or phrase.

Sharp teeth

Hungry

Always hungry

Ripping food apart

Killer fish.

This is an acrostic poem for SHARK.

Try writing your own acrostic poem.
Choose a short word to start with.
It can be something such as your
name, an animal, your pet's name,
or your favourite food.

Can you write an acrostic for TIGER?

T_____

I_____

G_____

E_____

R_____.

Shape poems

You can write your poem in any pattern or shape. Look at the poem below. It is about raindrops. It is written in the shape of a raindrop.

This is called a shape poem.

Drip, drip, drop, drop. Rain is falling. It doesn't stop. Drip, drip, drop, drop.

Try writing your own shape poem. Choose a word that gives you a strong shape to work with. You can find some good words in the list below.

Can you think of some other good shape words?

Shape words

heart

star

mountain

football

tree

Haikus

A **haiku** is a very short poem. It has only three **lines**. The first haikus were written in Japan hundreds of years ago. Haikus follow the strict rules below.

A **syllable** is a separate sound in a word.

Haiku rules

- **has three lines**
- **line 1 has 5 syllables**
- **line 2 has 7 syllables**
- **line 3 has 5 syllables**

Try writing your own haiku. Look closely at something, such as your pet, an object in your bedroom, or the flowers in your garden. Write down what you see.

Butterfly

Butterfly lands on

flower, flutters, drinks nectar,

flies away again.

A haiku is short enough to be said in one breath.

Free verse

Some poems do not follow any rules. They do not have to **rhyme**, and you can make the **lines** any length you want. This is called **free verse**.

The Farm
I like the farm,
With all its animals
and smells.
The ducks are best.
The goats are the smelliest.

Try writing a few lines of free verse.
Choose a subject, such as your
holiday or your favourite hobby.
Keep reading your poem out loud
to get the **rhythm** right.

Think carefully about where to put the line breaks.

Football

The whistle blows for kick-off.

I run down the field, fast as

the wind.

Dodging two players, I shoot!

The ball flies – it's a GOAL!

Writing a poem

You have done lots of thinking. Now, it is time to start writing your poem. You can choose a short poem, like a **haiku**, or write a poem that has several **verses**.

The Owl and the Pussycat is a famous poem.

Your poem can tell a story or describe something you have seen. It can be about a special memory or about your feelings. In fact, a poem can be about anything you want.

food   pirates

pets   holidays

animals   toys

friends

monsters

weather

Here are a few things you could write a poem about.

Top tips for writing poems

1. Read lots of different types of poems. The more you read, the better your own writing will become.

2. Read your poem when you have finished it. Check the spelling and make any changes you want. This might take a few times to get right.

3. Read your poem out loud. This will help you to check that the **rhythm** is strong and the **rhymes** work well.

4. Use your senses to help you. Choose words that help you write down what you see, hear, feel, taste, and smell.

5. If you are stuck for a rhyming word, write down the end sound and try each letter of the alphabet in front. Pick out the real words that you make.

6. If you are stuck for ideas, try some automatic writing. Write down whatever comes into your head. Then turn it into a poem.

7. Collect all of your poems in a book or on the computer. You don't have to let anyone read them if you don't want them to.

8. Keep practising! Writing is just like learning to cook. You need to keep practising.

Glossary

alliteration using words that start with the same letters or sounds

beat pattern of sounds that is repeated regularly

fiction writing that is about made-up people or things

free verse poem that does not follow any rules

haiku short poem with only three lines. Each line has a set number of syllables.

limerick funny, five-line nonsense poem

line part of a poem that can be a sentence or part of a sentence

mind mapping thinking of everything you can about a subject

non-fiction writing that is about real people or things

rhyme when the ends of two words sound the same

rhythm pattern of sounds

riddle poem that gives clues so that the reader can guess the answer

syllable a separate sound in a word

verse group of several lines in a poem

Find out more

Books

Getting to Grips with Grammar series by Anita Ganeri, (Raintree Publishing, 2012)

How to Write Poems, Wes Magee (QED Publishing, 2008)

Websites

www.bbc.co.uk/schools/ks1bitesize/literacy

www.bbc.co.uk/schools/ks2bitesize/english/writing

Index